Hal•Leonard

INSTRUMENTAL PLAY-ALONG

AUDIO ACCESS INCLUDED

PLAYBACK+
Speed • Pitch • Balance • Loop

TRUMPET

A Charlie Brown Christmas

```
||||| ||| ||||| ||| ||||
T0079324
```

Audio arrangements by Peter Deneff

To access audio, visit:
www.halleonard.com/mylibrary

Enter Code
4505-2754-5350-9557

ISBN 978-1-70514-649-1

HAL•LEONARD®

Visit Hal Leonard Online at
www.halleonard.com

Contact us:
Hal Leonard
7777 West Bluemound Road
Milwaukee, WI 53213
Email: info@halleonard.com

In Europe, contact:
Hal Leonard Europe Limited
42 Wigmore Street
Marylebone, London, W1U 2RN
Email: info@halleonardeurope.com

In Australia, contact:
Hal Leonard Australia Pty. Ltd.
4 Lentara Court
Cheltenham, Victoria, 3192 Australia
Email: info@halleonard.com.au

CONTENTS

4   **Christmas Is Coming**

6   **The Christmas Song**
(Chestnuts Roasting on an Open Fire)

7   **Christmas Time Is Here**

8   **Linus and Lucy**

9   **My Little Drum**

10 **O Tannenbaum**

11 **Skating**

12 **What Child Is This**

CHRISTMAS IS COMING

TRUMPET

By VINCE GUARALDI

THE CHRISTMAS SONG
(Chestnuts Roasting on an Open Fire)

TRUMPET

Music and Lyric by MEL TORMÉ
and ROBERT WELLS

CHRISTMAS TIME IS HERE

TRUMPET

Words by LEE MENDELSON
Music by VINCE GUARALDI

LINUS AND LUCY

TRUMPET

By VINCE GUARALDI

MY LITTLE DRUM

TRUMPET

By VINCE GUARALDI

O TANNENBAUM

TRUMPET

Traditional
Arranged by VINCE GUARALDI

SKATING

By VINCE GUARALDI

TRUMPET

WHAT CHILD IS THIS

TRUMPET

Traditional
Arranged by VINCE GUARALDI

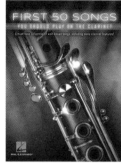

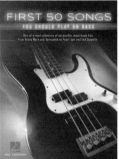

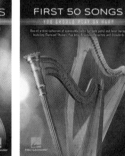

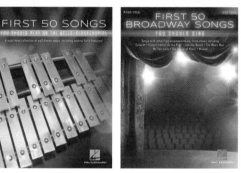

101 SONGS

BIG COLLECTIONS OF FAVORITE SONGS ARRANGED FOR SOLO INSTRUMENTALISTS.

101 BROADWAY SONGS

00154199 Flute.............$14.99
00154200 Clarinet.......$14.99
00154201 Alto Sax........$14.99
00154202 Tenor Sax....$14.99
00154203 Tumpet.........$14.99
00154204 Horn............$14.99
00154205 Trombone..$14.99
00154206 Violin...........$14.99
00154207 Viola.......................................$14.99
00154208 Cello..$14.99

101 DISNEY SONGS

00244104 Flute.............$14.99
00244106 Clarinet.......$14.99
00244107 Alto Sax.......$14.99
00244108 Tenor Sax...$14.99
00244109 Tumpet........$14.99
00244112 Horn.............$14.99
00244120 Trombone...$14.99
00244121 Violin.............$14.99
00244125 Viola.......................................$14.99
00244126 Cello..$14.99

101 MOVIE HITS

00158087 Flute.............$14.99
00158088 Clarinet.......$14.99
00158089 Alto Sax......$14.99
00158090 Tenor Sax...$14.99
00158091 Tumpet.........$14.99
00158092 Horn.............$14.99
00158093 Trombone...$14.99
00158094 Violin...........$14.99
00158095 Viola.......................................$14.99
001580 Cello..$14.99

101 CHRISTMAS SONGS

00278637 Flute.............$14.99
00278638 Clarinet.......$14.99
00278639 Alto Sax......$14.99
00278640 Tenor Sax..$14.99
00278641 Tumpet.........$14.99
00278642 Horn............$14.99
00278643 Trombone...$14.99
00278644 Violin...........$14.99
00278645 Viola.......................................$14.99
00278646 Cello..$14.99

101 HIT SONGS

00194561 Flute..............$14.99
00197182 Clarinet.........$14.99
00197183 Alto Sax.......$14.99
00197184 Tenor Sax.....$14.99
00197185 Tumpet.........$14.99
00197186 Horn.............$14.99
00197187 Trombone.....$14.99
00197188 Violin.............$14.99
00197189 Viola.......................................$14.99
00197190 Cello..$14.99

101 POPULAR SONGS

00224722 Flute.............$14.99
00224723 Clarinet.......$14.99
00224724 Alto Sax......$14.99
00224725 Tenor Sax...$14.99
00224726 Tumpet........$14.99
00224727 Horn.............$14.99
00224728 Trombone...$14.99
00224729 Violin...........$14.99
00224730 Viola.......................................$14.99
00224731 Cello..$14.99

101 CLASSICAL THEMES

00155315 Flute...............$14.99
00155317 Clarinet.........$14.99
00155318 Alto Sax........$14.99
00155319 Tenor Sax.....$14.99
00155320 Tumpet.........$14.99
00155321 Horn...............$14.99
00155322 Trombone..$14.99
00155323 Violin.............$14.99
00155324 Viola.......................................$14.99
0000155325 Cello..$14.99

101 JAZZ SONGS

00146363 Flute..............$14.99
00146364 Clarinet.........$14.99
00146366 Alto Sax.......$14.99
00146367 Tenor Sax....$14.99
00146368 Tumpet.........$14.99
00146369 Horn.............$14.99
00146370 Trombone...$14.99
00146371 Violin.............$14.99
00146372 Viola.......................................$14.99
00146373 Cello..$14.99

101 MOST BEAUTIFUL SONGS

00291023 Flute.............$14.99
00291041 Clarinet.......$14.99
00291042 Alto Sax.......$14.99
00291043 Tenor Sax...$14.99
00291044 Tumpet........$14.99
00291045 Horn.............$14.99
00291046 Trombone...$14.99
00291047 Violin.............$14.99
00291048 Viola.......................................$14.99
00291049 Cello..$14.99

See complete song lists and sample pages at www.halleonard.com

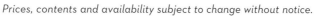

HAL•LEONARD®
www.halleonard.com